Healthy Plant-Based Diet Recipes

Plant-Based Diet Cookbook with Easy and Delicious Plant Based Recipes

Marlyn Moore

TABLE OF CONTENTS

INTRODUCTION

The plant based diet is becoming more and more popular as people strive to live a healthier lifestyle. Many people are still looking for ways to reduce their carbon footprint while also improving their overall health. The plant based diet has been gaining popularity for many years and there is a lot of information available about how to attain success on this eating plan.

This book was written with people like you in mind. There are multiple reasons for adopting a plant based diet, from helping our planet, to improving our health, to reducing our carbon footprint. These are some of the reasons people have for choosing a plant based diet, but they are not the only benefits.

This book is designed to give you with everything needed to make a successful change to your eating habits. You can cut out meat and dairy products completely and find yourself full of energy. This book will take you step by step through how changing your diet can happen in the most efficient way possible. You will learn about the various types of foods available for vegetarians as well as how to cook them and create delicious meals. It will also teach you about many benefits including weight loss, energy increase, and increased life span.

This book is designed to be a quick reference that you can turn to when you need advice on everything from cooking to what foods are the most beneficial for your body.

This book provides information that is both educational and fun for every member of the family. Not only will you learn about the plant based diet, but there are also some interesting stories of people practicing this type of lifestyle. You will want to keep this book on your coffee table and refer back to it whenever you need information on how to live a healthy life.

Information is power and the more we have, the better off we will be. This book was designed to provide an abundance of easy to understand information on every aspect of the plant based diet. It is written in a fun way that will keep people coming back for more information.

If you are looking to change the way you eat for your own health, the way you shop, or just want to share your passion with family and friends, this book is for you. You may be amazed at how much food is available and what it can do for your body. It is a great alternative to the standard "high carb" diet that has become so popular over the past few years.

This book was designed to provide information in an easy to understand manner that anyone can use. If you are looking for a change in the way you eat, this book can be your stepping stone into a new life of vibrant health and happiness. You will learn about all of the benefits of a plant based diet in a way that is both educational and fun.

This book is filled with a lot of tips and information making it perfect for anyone who is really interested in learning more about living a healthier lifestyle. You will learn all of the great benefits that come from following a plant based diet as you read through the various information that this book provides. This book was designed to be a quick reference guide that you can refer back to over and over again, to help you stay on track with your new eating habits. You will learn everything you need to know about adopting this type of diet including why it is important, the many benefits, and how to incorporate it into your life.

It doesn't matter if you are a vegetarian or not when reading this book. A large majority of people are becoming interested in a plant based diet and many are finding that it is the best way for them to live. Even if you are not planning on making a drastic change, knowing what is available and how to incorporate it into your current diet can have huge benefits. This book will take you step by step through all of the elements needed to make this healthy change in your life.

There's a lot of information packed into these pages and it has been written in a way that makes this process fun and exciting. It has been designed for anyone who is interested in learning more about living a healthier lifestyle using the plant based diet as their guide.

BREAKFAST

1. Orange Butter Crepes

Preparation Time: 5-15 minutes

Cooking Time: 30 minutes

Servings: 4

INGREDIENTS

- 2 tbsp flax seed powder + 6 tbsp water
- 1 tsp vanilla extract
- 1 tsp pure date sugar
- ¼ tsp salt
- 2 cups almond flour
- 1½ cups oat milk
- ½ cup melted plant butter
- 3 tbsp fresh orange juice
- 3 tbsp plant butter for frying

DIRECTIONS

1. In a medium bowl, mix the flax seed powder with 1 cup water and allow thickening for 5 minutes to make the flax egg. Whisk in the vanilla, date sugar, and salt.

2. Pour in a quarter cup of almond flour and whisk, then a quarter cup of oat milk, and mix until no lumps remain. Repeat the mixing process with the remaining almond flour and almond milk in the same quantities until exhausted.

3. Mix in the plant butter, orange juice, and half of the water until the mixture is runny like that of pancakes. Add the remaining water until the mixture is lighter. Brush a large non-stick skillet with some butter and place over medium heat to melt.

4. Pour 1 tablespoon of the batter in the pan and swirl the skillet quickly and all around to coat the pan with the batter. Cook until the batter is dry and golden brown beneath, about 30 seconds.

5. Use a spatula to carefully flip the crepe and cook the other side until golden brown too. Fold the crepe onto a plate and set aside. Repeat making more crepes with the remaining batter until exhausted. Drizzle some maple syrup on the crepes and serve.

NUTRITION: Calories 379 Fats 35. 6g Carbs 14.8g Protein 5.6g

2. Raspberry Raisin Muffins with Orange Glaze

Preparation Time: 5-15 minutes

Cooking Time: 40 minutes

Servings: 4

INGREDIENTS

For the muffins:

- 2 tbsp flax seed powder + 6 tbsp water
- 2 cups whole-wheat flour
- 1½ tsp baking powder
- A pinch salt
- ½ cup plant butter, room temperature
- 1 cup pure date sugar
- ½ cup oat milk
- 2 tsp vanilla extract
- 1 lemon, zested
- 1 cup dried raspberries

For the orange glaze:

- 2 tbsp orange juice
- 1 cup pure date sugar

DIRECTIONS

1. Preheat oven to 400 F and grease 6 muffin cups with cooking spray. In a small bowl, mix the flax seed powder with water and allow thickening for 5 minutes to make the flax egg. In a medium bowl, mix the flour, baking powder, and salt. In another bowl, cream the

plant butter, date sugar, and flax egg. Mix in the oat milk, vanilla, and lemon zest.

2. Combine both mixtures, fold in raspberries, and fill muffin cups two-thirds way up with the batter. Bake until a toothpick inserted comes out clean, 20-25 minutes.

3. In a medium bowl, whisk orange juice and date sugar until smooth. Remove the muffins when ready and transfer to a wire rack to cool. Drizzle the glaze on top to serve.

NUTRITION: Calories 700 Fats 25. 5g Carbs 115 1g Protein 10.5g

3. <u>Berry Cream Compote Over Crepes</u>

Preparation Time: 5-15 minutes

Cooking Time: 35 minutes

Servings: 4

INGREDIENTS

For the berry cream:

- 1 knob plant butter
- 2 tbsp pure date sugar
- 1 tsp vanilla extract
- ½ cup fresh blueberries
- ½ cup fresh raspberries

- ½ cup whipped coconut cream

For the crepes:

- 2 tbsp flax seed powder + 6 tbsp water
- 1 tsp vanilla extract
- 1 tsp pure date sugar
- ¼ tsp salt
- 2 cups almond flour
- 1 ½ cups almond milk
- 1 ½ cups water
- 3 tbsp plant butter for frying

DIRECTIONS

1. Melt butter in a pot over low heat and mix in the date sugar, and vanilla. Cook until the sugar melts and then, toss in berries. Allow softening for 2 3 minutes. Set aside to cool.

2. In a medium bowl, mix the flax seed powder with water and allow thickening for 5 minutes to make the flax egg. Whisk in the vanilla, date sugar, and salt.

3. Pour in a quarter cup of almond flour and whisk, then a quarter cup of almond milk, and mix until no lumps remain. Repeat the mixing process with the remaining almond flour and almond milk in the same quantities until exhausted.

4. Mix in 1 cup of water until the mixture is runny like that of pancakes and add the remaining water until the mixture is lighter. Brush a large non-stick skillet with some butter and place over medium heat to melt.

5. Pour 1 tablespoon of the batter in the pan and swirl the skillet quickly and all around to coat the pan with the batter. Cook until the batter is dry and golden brown beneath, about 30 seconds.

6. Use a spatula to carefully flip the crepe and cook the other side until golden brown too. Fold the crepe onto a plate and set aside. Repeat making more crepes with the remaining batter until exhausted. Plate the crepes, top with the whipped coconut cream and the berry compote. Serve immediately.

NUTRITION: Calories 339 Fats 24. 5g Carbs 30g Protein 2.3g

MAINS

4. Mac and Cheese

Preparation Time: 10-75 minutes

Cooking Time: 20 minutes

Servings: 4

INGREDIENTS

- 8 oz. whole-grain macaroni elbows, cooked
- 1 head of broccoli, florets
- 1 ½ tablespoons avocado oil
- 1 onion, chopped
- 1 cup potato, peeled and grated

- 3 cloves garlic, minced
- ½ teaspoon garlic powder
- ½ teaspoon onion powder
- ½ teaspoon dry mustard powder
- 1 small pinch red pepper flakes
- ⅔ cup raw cashews
- 1 cup water, or more if needed
- ¼ cup nutritional yeast
- 3 teaspoons apple cider vinegar
- salt

DIRECTIONS

1. Place a large pot over medium heat. Add salt and water and bring to a boil.
2. Add broccoli and cook for 5 minutes. Once done, drain excess liquid and set aside in a large mixing bowl.
3. Place a large skillet over medium heat. Add oil.
4. Add onion, salt and cook for about 5 minutes.
5. Add potatoes, garlic, garlic powder, onion powder, mustard powder, salt, red pepper flakes and cook for 60 seconds.
6. Add cashews, water, bring mixture to a simmer, reduce the heat and let it cook until potatoes are tender. Remove from the heat.
7. Pour the mixture into a food processor, add nutritional yeast, vinegar and pulse until the mixture is smooth, adding water if necessary.
8. Serve cooked pasta in bowls, topped with the blended mixture.

NUTRITION: Calories:680, Total Fat:71.8g, Saturated Fat:20.9g, Total Carbs:10g, Dietary Fiber:7g, Sugar:2g, Protein:3g, Sodium:525mg

5. Butternut Squash Linguine with Fried Sage

Preparation Time: 10-75 minutes

Cooking Time: 25 minutes

Servings: 4

INGREDIENTS

- 3 cups butternut squash, peeled, seeded, and chopped
- 2 cups vegetable broth
- 12 oz. whole grain fettucine, cooked, 1 cup cooking liquid saved
- 1 onion, chopped
- 2 garlic cloves, pressed
- 2 tablespoons olive oil
- 1 tablespoon fresh sage, chopped
- ⅛ teaspoon red pepper flakes
- salt and pepper

DIRECTIONS

1. Place a large pan over medium heat. Add oil.
2. Add sage and cook it until crispy. Season with salt and set aside.
3. Return the same pan to medium heat, add butternut, onion, garlic, red pepper flakes, salt and pepper. Cook for about 10 minutes.
4. Add broth and bring to a boil, then reduce the heat and let it cook for 20 minutes.
5. Place a pot of salty water over medium heat.

6. Cool the squash mixture and blend the mixture until smooth with a mixer.

7. Add pasta, ¼ cup reserved pasta liquid to the pan, return pan to medium heat and cook for 3 minutes.

NUTRITION: Calories: 140 Cal Fat: 0.9 g Carbs: 27.1 g Protein: 6.3 g Fiber: 6.2 g

6. Paella

Preparation Time: 10-75 minutes

Cooking Time: 1 hour

Servings: 6

INGREDIENTS

- 15 oz. diced tomatoes, drained
- 2 cups short-grain brown rice
- 1 ½ cups cooked chickpeas
- 3 cups vegetable broth
- ⅓ cup dry white wine
- 1 14 oz. artichokes, drained and chopped
- ½ cup Kalamata olives, pitted and halved
- ¼ cup parsley, chopped
- ½ cup peas
- 3 tablespoons extra-virgin olive oil, divided

- 1 onion, chopped
- 6 garlic cloves, pressed or minced
- 2 teaspoons smoked paprika
- ½ teaspoon saffron threads, crumbled
- 2 bell peppers, stemmed, seeded and sliced
- 2 tablespoons lemon juice
- salt and pepper

DIRECTIONS

1. Preheat the oven to 350F.
2. Place a large skillet over medium heat and add 2 tablespoons oil.
3. Add onion, salt and cook for 5 minutes.
4. Add garlic, paprika and cook for ½ a minute.
5. Add tomatoes and stir well. Cook until the mixture starts to thicken.
6. Add rice and cook for 1 minute while stirring.
7. Add chickpeas, broth, wine, saffron and salt to taste. Increase the heat and bring the mixture to a boil. Remove from the heat.
8. Cover and immediately transfer to an oven on lower rack. Bake for 1 hour.
9. Prepare a baking sheet by lining it with parchment paper. Combine artichokes, peppers, olives, 1 tablespoon olive oil, salt and pepper. Mix well and roast vegetables on the upper rack in the oven for 45 minutes.
10. Add parsley and lemon juice to the baking pan and mix well.

11. Sprinkle the roasted vegetables and peas on the baked rice.

NUTRITION: Calories: 140 Cal Fat: 0.9 g Carbs: 27.1 g Protein: 6.3 g Fiber: 6.2 g

7. Spicy Thai Peanut Sauce Over Roasted Sweet Potatoes and Rice

Preparation Time: 10-75 minutes

Cooking Time: 1 hour 30 minutes

Servings: 4

INGREDIENTS

For the spicy Thai peanut sauce:

- ½ cup creamy peanut butter
- ¼ cup reduced-sodium tamari
- 3 tablespoons apple cider vinegar
- 2 tablespoons honey or maple syrup
- 1 teaspoon grated fresh ginger
- 2 cloves garlic, pressed
- ¼ teaspoon red pepper flakes
- 2 tablespoons water

For the roasted vegetables:

- 2 sweet potatoes, peeled and sliced
- 1 bell pepper, cored, deseeded, and sliced
- about 2 tablespoons coconut oil (or olive oil)
- ¼ teaspoon cumin powder
- salt

For the rice and garnishes:

- 1 ¼ cup jasmine brown rice
- 2 green onions, sliced
- a handful of cilantro, torn
- a handful of peanuts, crushed

DIRECTIONS

1. Place a pot of water on medium heat and bring it to a boil.
2. Preheat the oven to 425F.
3. On a rimmed baking sheet, mix sweet potato, 1 tablespoon coconut oil, cumin and salt. Roast in the middle rack for about 35 minutes.
4. On another baking sheet, mix bell pepper with 1 teaspoon coconut oil, salt and mix well, Roast on the top rack for about 20 minutes until tender.
5. When water is boiling in the pot add rice and mix well. Cook for about 30 minutes and drain excess liquid. Once done, cover and let it sit for 10 minutes, fluff it after.
6. Mix sauce ingredients in a small bowl and set aside.
7. Divide rice, roasted vegetables in bowls and top with sauce, green onions, cilantro and peanuts before serving.

NUTRITION: Calories: 680, Total Fat:71.8g, Saturated Fat:20.9g, Total Carbs:10g, Dietary Fiber:7g, Sugar:2g, Protein:3g, Sodium:525mg

8. Butternut Squash Chipotle Chili With Avocado

Preparation Time: 10-75 minutes

Cooking Time: 20 minutes

Servings: 4

INGREDIENTS

- 3 cups black beans, cooked
- 14 oz. can diced tomatoes, including the liquid
- 2 cups vegetable broth
- 1 onion, chopped
- 2 bell peppers, chopped
- 1 small butternut squash, cubed
- 4 garlic cloves, minced
- 2 tablespoons olive oil
- 1 tablespoon chili powder
- ½ tablespoon chopped chipotle pepper in adobo
- 1 teaspoon ground cumin
- ¼ teaspoon ground cinnamon
- 1 bay leaf
- 2 avocados, diced
- 3 corn tortillas for crispy tortilla strips
- salt

DIRECTIONS

1. Place a stockpot over medium heat. Add oil.
2. Add and cook onion, bell peppers and butternut squash for about 5 minutes.

3. Reduce the heat, add garlic, chili powder, ½ tablespoon chopped chipotle peppers, cumin and cinnamon. Cook for ½ a minute.
4. Add bay leaves, black beans, tomatoes and their juices and broth. Mix well. Cook for about 1 hour. Remove bay leaf when done cooking.
5. Slice corn tortillas into thin little strips.
6. Place a pan over medium heat and add olive oil. Add tortilla strips and season with salt. Cook until crispy for about 7 minutes. Remove from the heat and place in a bowl covered with paper towel to drain excess oil.
7. Serve chili in bowls, topped with crispy tortilla chips and avocado.

NUTRITION: Calories: 140 Cal Fat: 0.9 g Carbs: 27.1 g Protein: 6.3 g Fiber: 6.2 g

9. Chickpea Biryani

Preparation Time: 10-75 minutes

Cooking Time: 40 minutes

Servings: 6

INGREDIENTS

- 4 cups veggie stock
- 2 cups basmati rice, rinsed
- 1 can chickpeas, drained, rinsed
- ½ cup raisins
- 1 large onion, thinly sliced
- 2 cups thinly sliced veggies (bell pepper, zucchini and carrots)
- 3 garlic cloves, chopped
- 1 tablespoon ginger, chopped
- 1 tablespoon cumin
- 1 tablespoon coriander
- 1 teaspoon chili powder
- 1 teaspoon cinnamon
- ½ teaspoon cardamom
- ½ teaspoon turmeric
- 2 tablespoons olive oil
- 1 bay leaf
- salt

DIRECTIONS

1. Place a large skillet over medium high heat. Add oil.
2. Sauté onions for about 5 minutes.

3. Reduce the heat to medium, add vegetables, garlic and ginger. Cook for 5 minutes. Scoop 1 cup of this mixture and set aside.
4. Add spices, bay leaf and rice. Stir for about 1 minute.
5. Add stock and salt to taste.
6. Add chickpeas, raisins and 1 cup of vegetables. Bring the mixture to a simmer over high heat.
7. Lower the heat, cover tightly and let it simmer for ½ an hour. Remove from the heat when rice is done.

NUTRITION: Calories: 140 Cal Fat: 0.9 g Carbs: 27.1 g Protein: 6.3 g Fiber: 6.2 g

10. Chinese Eggplant

Preparation Time: 10-75 minutes

Cooking Time: 45 minutes

Servings: 4

INGREDIENTS

- 1 ½ lbs. eggplants, chopped
- 2 cups water
- 2 tablespoons cornstarch
- 4 tablespoons peanut oil
- 4 cloves garlic, chopped
- 2 teaspoons ginger, minced
- 10 dried red chilies
- salt

For the Szechuan sauce:

- 1 teaspoon Szechuan peppercorns
- ¼ cup soy sauce
- 1 tablespoon garlic chili paste
- 1 tablespoon sesame oil
- 1 tablespoon rice vinegar
- 1 tablespoon Chinese cooking wine
- 3 tablespoons coconut sugar
- ½ teaspoon five spice

DIRECTIONS

1. Place chopped eggplants in a shallow bowl. Add water and 2 teaspoons salt. Stir cover and let it sit for about 15 minutes.

2. Meanwhile place a small pan over medium heat. Toast the Szechuan peppercorns for about 2 minutes and crush them.
3. Add crushed peppercorns to a medium bowl, add soy, chili paste, sesame oil, rice vinegar, Chinese cooking vinegar, coconut sugar and five spice.
4. Drain excess liquid from the eggplants and toss in the corn starch.
5. Place a large skillet over medium heat, add eggplants and cook them until golden. Set aside.
6. Add 1 tablespoon of oil in the skillet placed over medium heat. Cook garlic and ginger for 2 minutes.
7. Add dried chilies and cook for 1 minute. Add the Szechuan sauce and bring the mixture to a simmer in 20 seconds.
8. Add back eggplants and cook for about 60 seconds.

NUTRITION: Calories: 680, Total Fat:71.8g, Saturated Fat:20.9g, Total Carbs:10g, Dietary Fiber:7g, Sugar:2g, Protein:3g, Sodium:525mg

11. Black Pepper Tofu with Bok Choy

Preparation Time: 10-75 minutes

Cooking Time: 30 minutes

Servings: 2

INGREDIENTS

- 12 oz. firm tofu, cubed
- 1/3 cup corn starch for dredging
- 2 tablespoons coconut oil
- 1 teaspoon fresh cracked peppercorns
- 1 shallot, sliced
- 4 cloves garlic, chopped
- 6 oz. baby bok choy, sliced to 4 slices

For the black pepper sauce:

- 2 tablespoons soy sauce
- 2 tablespoons Chinese cooking wine
- 2 tablespoons water
- 1 teaspoon brown sugar
- ½ teaspoon fresh cracked peppercorns
- 1 teaspoon chili paste

DIRECTIONS

1. In a small bowl, combine wok sauce ingredients and mix well until sugar dissolves. Set aside.
2. Place cornstarch in a shallow bowl and dredge tofu in the cornstarch. Set aside.
3. Place a large skillet over medium heat. Heat 1 tablespoon coconut oil.

4. Add peppercorns and toast for about 1 minute.
5. Add tofu and cook on all sides for about 6 minutes. Set tofu aside.
6. Add the remaining coconut oil. Add shallots, garlic and bok choy. Cook for 8 minutes.
7. Add back the tofu and cook for less than a minute.

NUTRITION: Calories: 140 Cal Fat: 0.9 g Carbs: 27.1 g Protein: 6.3 g Fiber: 6.2 g

12. Spaghetti Alla Puttanesca

Preparation Time: 10-75 minutes

Cooking Time: 30 minutes

Servings: 4

INGREDIENTS

For the Puttanesca sauce:

- 28 oz. can chunky tomato sauce
- ⅓ cup chopped Kalamata olives
- ⅓ cup capers
- 1 tablespoon Kalamata olive brine
- 1 tablespoon caper brine
- 3 cloves garlic, minced
- ¼ teaspoon red pepper flakes
- 1 tablespoon olive oil
- ½ cup parsley leaves, chopped and divided
- salt and pepper

For the pasta:

- 8 oz. whole grain spaghetti
- 6 oz. zucchini noodles

DIRECTIONS

1. Place a medium skillet over medium heat.
2. Add tomato sauce, olives, capers, olive brine, caper brine, garlic and red pepper flakes. Bring the mixture to a boil, reduce the heat and let it simmer for 20 minutes. Remove from the heat and set aside.

3. Place a pot over medium heat. Add water, salt, spaghetti and cook as directed on package. When done, drain excess water.

4. Pour the sauce over pasta and mix well.

5. Add zucchini noodles before serving.

NUTRITION: Calories: 140 Cal Fat: 0.9 g Carbs: 27.1 g Protein: 6.3 g Fiber: 6.2 g

13. Thai Red Curry

Preparation Time: 10-75 minutes

Cooking Time: 40 minutes

Servings: 4

INGREDIENTS

- 1 ¼ cups brown jasmine rice, rinsed
- 1 tablespoon coconut oil
- 1 cup onion, chopped
- 1 tablespoon fresh ginger, ginger
- 2 cloves garlic, minced
- 1 red bell pepper, sliced
- 1 yellow bell pepper, sliced
- 3 carrots, peeled and sliced
- 2 tablespoons Thai red curry paste
- 1 14 oz. can coconut milk
- ½ cup water
- 1 ½ cups packed kale, chopped
- 1 ½ teaspoons coconut sugar
- 1 tablespoon tamari
- 2 teaspoons fresh lime juice

DIRECTIONS

1. Place a large pot over medium heat and add water. Bring it to a boil.
2. Add rice, salt and cook for 30 minutes. Remove from the heat, cover and let it sit for 10 minutes.
3. Place a large pan over medium heat. Add oil.
4. Cook onion and salt for about 5 minutes.

5. Add garlic, ginger and cook for about ½ a minute.
6. Add bell peppers, carrots and cook for about 5 minutes.
7. Add curry paste and cook for additional 2 minutes.
8. Add coconut milk, water, kale, sugar, tamari and lime juice. Remove from the heat.

NUTRITION: Calories:680, Total Fat:71.8g, Saturated Fat:20.9g, Total Carbs:10g, Dietary Fiber:7g, Sugar:2g, Protein:3g, Sodium:525mg

14. Thai Green Curry with Spring Vegetables

Preparation Time: 10-75 minutes

Cooking Time: 45 minutes

Servings:4

INGREDIENTS

- 1 cup brown basmati rice, rinsed
- 2 teaspoons coconut oil
- 1 onion, diced
- 1 tablespoon fresh ginger, chopped
- 2 cloves garlic, chopped
- 2 cups asparagus, sliced
- 1 cup carrots, peeled and sliced
- 2 tablespoons Thai green curry paste
- 14 oz. full-fat coconut milk (I used full-fat coconut milk for a richer curry)
- ½ cup water
- 1 ½ teaspoons coconut sugar
- 2 cups packed baby spinach, chopped
- 1 ½ teaspoons fresh lime juice
- 1 ½ teaspoons tamari
- salt

DIRECTIONS

1. Place a pot over medium heat. Add water and bring it to a boil.

2. Add rice, salt to taste and cook for 30 minutes. When done, cover the rice and set aside for more than 10 minutes.
3. Place a large skillet over medium heat. Add oil.
4. Cook onion, garlic, ginger and a pinch of salt.
5. Add asparagus, carrots and cook for 3 minutes.
6. Add curry paste and cook for additional 2 minutes.
7. Add coconut milk, ½ cup water, sugar and bring this mixture to a simmer. Reduce the heat and let it cook for 10 minutes until vegetables are tender.
8. Add spinach and let it cook for ½ a minute. Remove from the heat and season with rice vinegar and tamari.

NUTRITION: Calories: 140 Cal Fat: 0.9 g Carbs: 27.1 g Protein: 6.3 g Fiber: 6.2 g

15. Tamarind Potato Curry

Preparation Time: 10-75 minutes

Cooking Time: 1 hour

Servings: 4

INGREDIENTS

- 26.5 oz. potatoes, peeled and cubed
- 1 onion
- 1 garlic clove
- 1-inch ginger, chopped
- 1 green chilli, chopped
- oil for frying
- 1 teaspoon cumin seeds
- ½ teaspoon fennel seeds
- 1 teaspoon ground coriander
- 1 teaspoon chilli powder
- 14 oz. plum tomatoes
- 2 teaspoon brown sugar
- 2 tablespoons tamarind paste
- 1 handful coriander leaves
- rice or naan bread, to serve

DIRECTIONS

1. Place a pot of water over medium heat. Add salt and potatoes. Bring to a boil.
2. Place onion, garlic, ginger, chili, and 2 tablespoons water in a food processor. Pulse until smooth.
3. Place a pan over medium heat. Add oil.
4. Toast cumin and fennel seeds until they pop.

5. Add spices, puree and cook for 5 minutes.

6. Add tomatoes, sugar, tamarind and let it simmer for 10 minutes.

7. Add potatoes and some water. Cover and let it cook until tender.

8. Serve with rice or naan bread.

NUTRITION: Calories: 140 Cal Fat: 0.9 g Carbs: 27.1 g Protein: 6.3 g Fiber: 6.2 g

16. West African Stew with Sweet Potato and Greens

Preparation Time: 10-75 minutes

Cooking Time: 1 hour

Servings: 4

INGREDIENTS

- 1/5 cup crunchy peanut butter
- 1/3 cup coconut cream
- 3 cups vegetable stock
- 21 oz. sweet potatoes, cubed
- 2 cups okra, halved
- 1 cup loosely packed kale, chopped
- 2 onions, 1 roughly chopped and 1 diced
- 1-inch ginger, chopped
- 3 garlic cloves
- 1 scotch bonnet chilli
- 4 tablespoons tomato purée
- sunflower oil
- 2 teaspoons coriander seeds, toasted and crushed
- 2 teaspoons ground cumin
- salt

DIRECTIONS

1. Combine roughly chopped onion, ginger, garlic, scotch bonnet, tomato puree and peanut butter in a blender. Blend for 1 minute until paste forms.
2. Place a cast iron pan over medium heat. Add 2 tablespoons sunflower oil.

3. Add diced onions and cook for 5 minutes. Season with salt.
4. Add spices, peanut sauce and cook for 5 minutes.
5. Add coconut cream, stock and bring it to a simmer for about 10 minutes.
6. Add cubed sweet potatoes, cover and cook for about 15 minutes.
7. Add okra, kale and cook for 10 additional minutes.
8. Remove from heat before serving.

NUTRITION: Calories: 680, Total Fat: 71.8g, Saturated Fat:20.9g, Total Carbs:10g, Dietary Fiber:7g, Sugar:2g, Protein:3g, Sodium:525mg

17. Kale Slaw

Preparation Time: 10-75 minutes

Cooking Time: 15 minutes

Servings: 4

INGREDIENTS

- 1 small bunch kale, chopped
- ½ small head cabbage, shredded
- ¼ onion, thinly sliced
- ¼ cup tender herbs (cilantro, basil, parsley, chives)
- ¼ cup olive oil
- 4 tablespoons lemon juice
- 2 garlic cloves, minced
- salt, pepper and chili flakes

DIRECTIONS

1. Combine kale, cabbage, herbs and onions in a large bowl.
2. Add olive oil, lemon juice, minced garlic, salt, pepper and mix well.
3. Add chili flakes, toss well before serving.

NUTRITION: Calories: 140 Cal Fat: 0.9 g Carbs: 27.1 g Protein: 6.3 g Fiber: 6.2 g

18. Salisbury Steak and Mushroom Gravy

Preparation Time: 30 Minutes

Cooking Time: 30-120 minutes

Servings: 4

INGREDIENTS

- 4 palm-sized pieces beef seitan
- 1 1/2 tablespoons vegan chicken-flavored bouillon
- 8 ounces mushrooms, chopped
- 1/2 teaspoon garlic powder
- 1/2 teaspoon basil
- 1 bay leaf
- 1/8 teaspoon celery salt
- 1/8 teaspoon seasoned salt
- 1/4 teaspoon pepper
- 1 cup water
- 1 cup nondairy milk
- 2 tablespoons olive oil
- 1/2 cup plus 3 tablespoons flour

DIRECTIONS

1. Make a coating for the seitan by mixing the garlic powder, celery salt, ½ cup flour, basil, seasoned salt, and pepper in a bowl. Make sure seitan is wet before coating it with the flour mixture.
2. Heat the oil in the instant pot on the sauté setting. Brown the seitan steaks on each side, then set aside.
3. Add the water, mushrooms, bay leaf, and bouillon to the instant pot, then place the seitan on top. Seal the lid

and cook on high 4 minutes, before letting the pressure release naturally.

4. Remove the lid and discard the bay leaf. Return to the sauté setting.
5. Remove the steaks, then stir in the nondairy milk. Add the flour to thicken the gravy, then add the steaks. Simmer for 10 minutes. Add additional flour if needed.
6. Serve with a side of mashed potatoes smothered in your mushroom gravy.

NUTRITION: Calories: 140 Cal Fat: 0.9 g Carbs: 27.1 g Protein: 6.3 g Fiber: 6.2 g

19. Savory Spinach and Mushroom Crepes

Preparation Time: 60 Minutes

Cooking Time: 30-120 minutes

Servings: 4

INGREDIENTS

For the crepes:

- 1 ¾ cup rolled oats
- 1 tsp pink Himalayan salt
- 1 ½ cup soy milk
- 2 tbsp olive oil
- 1 tbsp almond butter
- ½ tsp nutmeg
- 2 tbsp egg replacement

For the filling:

- 1 lb button mushrooms
- 10 oz fresh spinach, finely chopped
- 4 oz crumbled tofu
- 1 tbsp chia seeds
- 1 tbsp fresh rosemary, finely chopped
- 1 garlic clove, crushed
- 2 tbsp olive oil

DIRECTIONS

1. First, prepare the crepes. Combine all dry ingredients in a large bowl. Add milk, butter, nutmeg, olive oil, and egg replacement. Mix well with a hand mixer on high

speed. Transfer to a food processor and process until completely smooth.

2. Grease a large non-stick pancake pan with some oil. Pour 1 cup of the mixture into the pan and cook for one minute on each side.

3. Plug in your instant pot and press the 'Sauté' button. Grease the stainless steel insert with some oil and add mushrooms. Cook for 5 minutes, stirring constantly.

4. Now add spinach, tofu, rosemary, and garlic. Continue to cook for another 5 minutes.

5. Remove the mixture from the pot and stir in chia seeds. Let it sit for 10 minutes.

6. Meanwhile, grease a small baking pan with some oil and line with parchment paper.

7. Divide the mushroom mixture between crepes and roll up. Gently transfer to a prepared baking pan.

8. Wrap the pan with aluminum foil and set aside.

9. Pour 1 cup of water in your instant pot and set the steam rack. Put the pan on top and seal the lid. Press the 'Manual' button and set the timer for 10 minutes.

10. When done, release the pressure naturally, and open the lid.

11. Optionally, sprinkle with some dried oregano before serving.

NUTRITION: Calories: 680, Total Fat:71.8g, Saturated Fat:20.9g, Total Carbs:10g, Dietary Fiber:7g, Sugar:2g, Protein:3g, Sodium:525mg

20. Stuffed Sweet Onions

Preparation Time: 45 Minutes

Cooking Time: 30-120 minutes

Servings: 5

INGREDIENTS

- 10 medium-sized sweet onions
- 1 lb portobello mushrooms, chopped
- 1 medium-sized eggplant, finely chopped
- 3 tbsp olive oil
- 1 tbsp dried mint
- 1 tsp cayenne pepper
- ½ tsp cumin powder
- 1 tsp salt
- ½ cup tomato paste
- ¼ cup fresh parsley, finely chopped

DIRECTIONS

1. Cut a ¼-inch slice from top of each onion and trim a small amount from the bottom end. This will make the onions stand upright. Place onions in a microwave-safe dish and add about 1 cup of water. Cover with a tight lid and microwave on High 2-3 minutes. Remove onions from a dish and cool slightly. Now carefully remove inner layers of onions with a sharp knife, leaving about ¼-inch onion shell.

2. In a large bowl, combine chopped mushrooms, eggplant, olive oil, mint, cayenne pepper, cumin

powder, salt, and tomato paste. Use 1 tablespoon of the mixture to fill the onions.

3. Grease the bottom of the stainless-steel insert with some oil and gently place onions. Add 2 cups of water or vegetable stock and seal the lid. Press the 'Manual' button and set the timer for 15 minutes.

4. When done, release the pressure naturally and open the lid. Sprinkle with parsley before serving.

NUTRITION: Calories: 140 Cal Fat: 0.9 g Carbs: 27.1 g Protein: 6.3 g Fiber: 6.2 g

21. Eggplant Casserole

Preparation Time: 50 Minutes

Cooking Time: 30-120 minutes

Servings: 4

INGREDIENTS

- 1 large eggplant, sliced
- 7 oz button mushrooms
- 2 large onions, finely chopped
- 2 large tomatoes, sliced
- 7 oz cherry tomatoes, sliced
- ½ cup almond butter
- ¼ cup-soaked cashews
- 2 tbsp egg replacement
- ¼ cup olive oil
- 1 tsp salt
- ½ tsp freshly ground black pepper

DIRECTIONS

1. Grease a round baking pan with two tablespoons of olive oil and set aside.
2. Plug in your instant pot and grease the stainless-steel insert with the remaining oil. Press the 'Sauté' button and add onions. Stir-fry until translucent. Now add mushrooms, salt, and pepper. Continue to cook for 3-4 minutes, stirring constantly.
3. Finally, add almond butter and cook until melted.

4. Remove the mixture from your pot and transfer to a medium-sized bowl. Add tomatoes, cherry tomatoes, soaked cashews, and egg replacement. Mix well.

5. Spread half of the eggplant slices over the prepared pan and top with the tomato mixture. Finish with the remaining eggplant and wrap tightly with aluminum foil.

6. Pour in 2 cups of water in your instant pot and set the steam rack. Put the pan on top and seal the lid. Set the steam release handle and press the 'Manual' button.

7. Set the timer for 25 minutes.

8. When done, perform a quick release and open the lid. Remove the pan and chill for a while before serving.

NUTRITION: Calories: 140 Cal Fat: 0.9 g Carbs: 27.1 g Protein: 6.3 g Fiber: 6.2 g

22. Corn Chowder

Preparation Time: 20 minutes

Cooking Time: 15-120 minutes

Servings: 4

INGREDIENTS

- 2 Tablespoons Vegan Butter
- 4 Scallions, chopped, use green tops and white bulbs and set aside separately
- 1 Sweet Red Bell Pepper, diced
- 2 Celery Stalks, diced
- 4 Cups Vegetable Broth
- 1 pound Red or New Potatoes, peeled and diced
- 4 Cups Corn Kernels, fresh from the cob is best, but frozen is okay
- 1 Bay Leaf
- 2 Teaspoons Sea Salt
- 2 Cups Unsweetened Plain Almond Milk
- 1/4 Teaspoon Black Pepper

DIRECTIONS

1. On sauté mode, add butter until melted.
2. Add the white bulbs of the scallions, red pepper, and celery. Cook until soft.
3. Add broth, potatoes, corn, and bay leaf.
4. Season with a pinch of salt.
5. Put instant pot on manual mode on high. Seal the lid and set to 10 minutes.

6. When done cooking, release the pressure and open when steam has evaporated.
7. Add almond milk and pepper. Stir.
8. Put instant pot in sauté mode and allow to boil for 2 minutes to thicken slightly.
9. Remove the bay leaf and stir in the green tops of the scallions.
10. Enjoy!

NUTRITION: Calories:680, Total Fat:71.8g, Saturated Fat:20.9g, Total Carbs:10g, Dietary Fiber:7g, Sugar:2g, Protein:3g, Sodium:525mg

23. Lemony Roasted Vegetable Risotto

Preparation Time: 30 minutes

Cooking Time: 15-120 minutes

Servings: 4

INGREDIENTS

- 3 1/2 Cups Butternut Squash, peeled, cubed
- 1/1/2 Cups Zucchini, diced
- 1 large Carrot, peeled, chopped
- 2 Tablespoons Olive Oil
- Sea Salt + Pepper to taste
- 1 Onion, diced
- 2 Garlic Cloves, minced
- 6 Cups Vegetable Broth
- 1 Tablespoon Vegan Butter
- 2 Cups Arborio Rice
- 1/2 Cup Baby Spinach
- 1 Teaspoon Lemon Zest
- 2 Tablespoons lemon juice, more to taste

DIRECTIONS

1. Preheat oven to 400 degrees F. Line a baking tray with parchment paper. Add butternut squash, zucchini, and carrot to the tray. Coat with 1 teaspoon of olive oil, salt, and pepper, toss well.

2. Roast in the oven for 15-20 minutes or until squash is soft when poked with a fork. When done, remove from oven and set aside.

3. Press saute mode on instant pot. Add remaining olive oil, and when hot, cook onions and garlic for 2-3 minutes or until onions become semitransparent.
4. Add rice and stir for 1-2 minutes to coat.
5. Add broth, and vegan butter. Stir to combine.
6. Turn the instant pot off. Cover and seal. Press manual button and adjust the time to 7 minutes.
7. When done cooking, release the pressure and stir well.
8. Return to saute mode, add spinach and roasted vegetables.
9. Stir until spinach has wilted. Taste and add salt and pepper as needed.
10. Top with lemon juice and zest.
11. Best when served fresh and warm.
12. Enjoy!

NUTRITION: Calories: 140 Cal Fat: 0.9 g Carbs: 27.1 g Protein: 6.3 g Fiber: 6.2 g

24. Thai Coconut Peanut Tofu

Preparation Time: 26 minutes

Cooking Time: 15-120 minutes

Servings: 4

INGREDIENTS

- 1 Cup Creamy Natural Peanut Butter
- 1 Can (about 1 1/2 CupsLight Coconut Milk
- 1/2 Cup Vegetable Broth
- 2 Teaspoons Curry Powder
- 2 Tablespoons Coconut Sugar
- 2 Teaspoons Ground Cumin Powder
- 1/4 Teaspoon Sea Salt, add more to taste
- 1-2 Tablespoons Coconut Oil (or Olive or Sesame Oil
- 1 Bunch Green Onions, sliced (reserve half for garnish
- 2 Tablespoons minced Fresh Ginger
- 1 Cup Carrots, shredded
- 1/4 Cup Roasted Cashews, salted or unsalted
- 1 Pinch Cayenne Pepper
- 2 Tablespoons Tamari (or Soy Sauce
- 3 Teaspoons Rice Vinegar
- 1 Package (200 GramsExtra-Firm Tofu, cubed
- 1 Lemon, juiced

DIRECTIONS

1. In a bowl, mix peanut butter, coconut milk, broth, curry powder, coconut sugar, cumin, and sea salt. Make sure ingredients are mixed completely. Set aside.

2. Press saute mode on instant pot. When it is hot, add the coconut oil, half of the green onions, ginger, and garlic.
3. Add a pinch of salt and saute for 2-3 minutes, stirring frequently.
4. Add the carrots, cashews, cayenne, and saute for 2 minutes more.
5. Add the peanut butter mixture into the pot and stir well.
6. Then add tamari or soy sauce and rice vinegar. Stir to combine.
7. Lastly, add tofu to the pot and mix.
8. Cover and turn off saute mode. Press the manual button, change pressure to high and let cook for 2 minutes.
9. Quick release when 2 minutes are done.
10. Return to saute mode and let simmer to let tofu infuse with flavor. Add more broth if too thick.
11. Add lemon juice and serve over rice, quinoa, or steamed vegetables.
12. Garnish with the rest of the green onions and enjoy!

NUTRITION: Calories: 140 Cal Fat: 0.9 g Carbs: 27.1 g Protein: 6.3 g Fiber: 6.2 g

25. Vegan Butter Curry Tofu

Preparation Time: 77 minutes

Cooking Time: 15-120 minutes

Servings: 4-5

INGREDIENTS

- 1 1/2 Cups Coconut Yogurt
- 4 Cloves Garlic, minced
- 1 Teaspoon Fresh Ginger, grated
- Sea Salt
- 1 Package Extra-Firm Tofu, cubed
- 1/2 Cup Vegan Butter
- 1 Teaspoon Cumin Seeds
- 1 Onion, diced
- 2 Teaspoons Garam Masala
- 2 Teaspoons Curry Powder
- 1 Teaspoon Paprika
- 1 Teaspoon Cinnamon
- 2 Teaspoons Cayenne (optional
- 1 6 Ounce Can Tomato Paste
- 1 14 Ounce Can Coconut Milk
- 1 Cup Vegetable Broth
- Cilantro, for garnish
- Cooked Jasmine or Basmati Rice
- Naan (optional

DIRECTIONS

1. In a bowl, make a marinade by mixing coconut yogurt, garlic, ginger, and sea salt. Add tofu and toss to coat. Refrigerate for 1 hour.
2. After marinade is ready, spread out tofu in a single layer on a baking sheet. Broil until tofu starts to turn brown on all sides, about 20 minutes, turning tofu ever 5 minutes. Set aside when done.
3. Turn on the instant pot to saute mode and melt butter.
4. Add cumin seeds and cook for 1 minute.
5. Add onions and cook until soft (2-3 minutes
6. Add garam masala, curry powder, paprika, cinnamon, and cayenne (optional). Stir.
7. Stir in tomato paste, coconut milk, and broth.
8. Set instant pot to manual mode and cook for 12 minutes.
9. When finished, let pressure naturally release for 5 minutes, then quick release.
10. Stir in tofu.
11. Top tofu and sauce over rice and garnish with cilantro and serve with naan (optional
12. Enjoy!

NUTRITION: Calories: 140 Cal Fat: 0.9 g Carbs: 27.1 g Protein: 6.3 g Fiber: 6.2 g

26. Thai Coconut Rice

Preparation Time: 30 minutes

Cooking Time: 15-120 minutes

Servings: 4

INGREDIENTS

- 1 Cup White Sticky Rice or Jasmine Rice, rinsed
- 1 1/2 Cups Water
- 1 14 Ounce Can Coconut Milk
- 1/2 Teaspoon Sea Salt
- 1/2 Teaspoon Organic Cane Sugar
- Sesame Seeds (optional

DIRECTIONS

1. Add 2 cups of water to inner pot and insert trivet.
2. In an oven-safe bowl add rice and 1 1/2 cups of water.
3. Place bowl on trivet, close lid and seal. Pressure cook on high for 15 minutes.
4. On a stovetop, simmer coconut milk, sugar, and salt.
5. When rice is done cooking, allow pressure to release naturally then quick release.
6. Open and remove bowl.
7. Pour half of the coconut sauce into the rice and stir well.
8. Top with sesame seeds optional and more coconut sauce.
9. Enjoy!

NUTRITION: Calories: 140 Cal Fat: 0.9 g Carbs: 27.1 g Protein: 6.3 g Fiber: 6.2 g

SIDES

27. Potato Chili

Preparation Time: 10 min

Cooking Time: 25 min

Servings: 2

INGREDIENTS

- ½ teaspoon olive oil
- ½ cup onion chopped
- ½ teaspoon garlic powder
- ½ teaspoon chili powder
- ½ teaspoon ground cumin
- 1 cup diced tomatoes
- ½ cup black beans rinsed and drained
- 1 medium red bell pepper seeded and diced
- 1 medium potato peeled and diced
- 1 teaspoon kosher salt
- ¼ cup frozen corn kernels

DIRECTIONS

1. Select Sauté and add the olive oil to the Instant Pot. Add the onions and garlic powder. Sauté for 2 minutes, or until the garlic powder is fragrant and the onion is soft and translucent.

2. Add the chili powder and ground cumin, followed by the tomatoes, black beans, red bell pepper, potato, corn, and salt. Stir well.

3. Cover, lock the lid, and flip the steam release handle to the Sealing position. Select Pressure Cook High and set the cook time for 15 minutes. When the cook time is complete, allow the pressure to release naturally about 20 minutes.
4. Remove the lid and ladle the chili into serving bowls. Serve hot.

NUTRITION: Calories 207, Total Fat 2. 1g, Saturated Fat 0. 3g, Cholesterol 0mg, Sodium 1207mg, Total Carbohydrate 41.4g, Dietary Fiber 8. 8g, Total Sugars 7 7g, Protein 8. 2g

28. Beans Baby Potato Curry

Preparation Time: 10 min

Cooking Time:30 min

Servings: 2

INGREDIENTS

- 1 small onion, chopped
- ½ teaspoon garlic, chopped finely
- 1 cup baby potatoes
- ½ tablespoon curry powder
- 2 cups water
- ½ cup pinto beans
- ½ cup milk
- ½ tablespoon honey
- Salt & pepper to taste
- ½ teaspoon chili pepper flakes
- 1 tablespoon arrowroot powder

DIRECTIONS

1. Set your Instant Pot to Sauté. Once hot, add a few drops of water and cook the onions until translucent, then add the garlic and cook for one minute longer. Press the Keep Warm/Cancel button.
2. Add everything to the Instant Pot except the arrowroot powder.
3. Set the Instant Pot to 20 minutes on Manual High pressure and allow the pressure to release naturally after this time.

4. Press Keep Warm/Cancel, remove the lid and press Sauté. Put the arrowroot into a small bowl or cup and mix into it a few tablespoons of water to make a thickness but pour slurry. Pour it into the Instant Pot stirring as you go.
5. Add salt and pepper to taste then cook for about 5 minutes until they are tender and the gravy has thickened.
6. Serve immediately.

NUTRITION: Calories342, Total Fat 2. 3g, Saturated Fat 1g, Cholesterol 5mg, Sodium 58mg, Total Carbohydrate 67.2g, Dietary Fiber 12. 1g, Total Sugars 10g, Protein 14. 2g

29. Butter Tofu with Soy Bean and Chickpeas

Preparation Time: 10 min

Cooking Time: 30 min

Servings: 2

INGREDIENTS

- 2 large ripe tomatoes
- ½ teaspoon garlic powder
- ½ teaspoon ginger powder
- ½ tablespoon hot green chili
- 1 cup water
- ¼ teaspoon garam masala
- 1/8 teaspoon paprika
- ¼ teaspoon salt
- ¼ cup soy beans
- ½ cup chickpeas
- ½ teaspoon honey
- ½ cup coconut cream
- Cilantro for garnish

DIRECTIONS

1. Blend the tomatoes, garlic powder, ginger powder, hot green chili with water until smooth.
2. Add pureed tomato mixture to the Instant Pot. Add soy beans, chickpeas, spices and salt. Close the lid and cook on Manual for 8 to 10 minutes. Quick release after 10 minutes.

3. Start the Instant Pot on Sauté. Add the coconut cream, Garam masala, honey and mix in. Bring to a boil, taste and adjust salt,. Add more paprika and salt if needed.
4. Serve with cilantro garnishing

NUTRITION: Calories 242, Total Fat 1. 3g, Saturated Fat 1. 5g, Cholesterol 5mg, Sodium 38mg, Total Carbohydrate 47.2g, Dietary Fiber 10. 1g, Total Sugars 10g, Protein 14. 2g.

30. Black Eyed Peas Curry with Jiggery

Preparation Time: 10 min

Cooking Time: 30 min

Servings: 2

INGREDIENTS

- ¼ cup dried black eyed peas, soaked in water for about 1-2 hours
- 2 cups water
- 1 dried curry leaves
- 1/8 teaspoon mustard seeds
- ½ teaspoon garlic powder
- 1/2 small onion, finely chopped
- 2 tablespoons tomato paste
- ½ teaspoon ground cumin
- 1 teaspoon ground coriander
- ¼ teaspoon ground turmeric
- 1 tablespoon jiggery
- 1 tablespoon fresh lemon juice
- Chili powder, to taste (optional
- 1 tablespoon avocado oil
- Salt
- Fresh cilantro, finely chopped

DIRECTIONS

1. Select the Sauté button into the Instant Pot and add avocado oil.
2. Once the oil is hot, add the mustard seeds and curry leaves. Fry for a few seconds until fragrant.

3. Add the onions and garlic powder. Sauté until fragrant and the onions start to become translucent. Be sure not to burn either. If you see this happening add more oil or turn down the sauté heat.

4. Quickly add the tomato paste, ground cumin, and ground coriander. Combine and cook for a minute mixing frequently.

5. Drain the soaked black eyed peas and add them into the Instant Pot.

6. Mix in the water, turmeric powder, chili powder, jiggery, fresh lemon juice, and salt.

7. Close the Instant Pot lid, select the Pressure Cook button to cook on High. Set the timer for about 13-15 minutes.

8. When the time is up, allow the pressure to release naturally.

9. Once the pressure has been released, remove the lid, and press the Sauté (normally Low) button again on the Instant Pot. The black eyed peas should be fully cooked.

10. Simmer for a few more minutes until the curry becomes thick.

11. Add salt to taste. Also feel free to adjust the amount of lemon juice and jiggery as needed.

12. Turn the Instant Pot off. Add freshly chopped cilantro and serve hot.

NUTRITION: Calories79, Total Fat 0. 9g, Saturated Fat 0. 2g, Cholesterol 0mg, Sodium 75mg, Total Carbohydrate 18g, Dietary Fiber 4. 7g, Total Sugars 8 2g, Protein 4g

31. Jackfruit with Beans Curry

Preparation Time: 10 min

Cooking Time: 20 min

Servings: 2

INGREDIENTS

- ½ tablespoon coconut oil
- ½ tablespoon curry powder
- ¼ teaspoon paprika
- ½ teaspoon cumin seeds
- ¼ teaspoon turmeric powder
- 1 sprigs fresh rosemary
- ½ cup onion, finely chopped
- 1 teaspoon garlic powder
- 1 teaspoon ginger powder
- 1 celery, chopped
- 1 cup jackfruit, drained and rinsed
- ½ cup pinto beans
- ½ medium zucchini, diced
- ½ cup full fat milk
- 1 cups vegetable broth
- 1/4 cup parsley leaves, chopped
- Salt, to taste

DIRECTIONS

1. Plug in your Instant Pot and press Sauté mode button. Add coconut oil, once heated add dry spices, curry powder, paprika, cumin seeds, turmeric powder, rosemary and cook for a minute stirring constantly.

2. Add onions, garlic powder, ginger powder, and celery and cook until for 2 minutes or until onions are soft. Add jackfruit, pinto beans, zucchini and stir to coat.
3. Add salt, milk, and vegetable broth.
4. Close Instant Pot lid and press Manual mode for 10 minutes. When finished, allow Instant Pot to natural release for 10 minutes. Carefully release the knob to release the remaining pressure. Remove lid, stir in parsley leaves, and check seasonings.
5. Serve.

NUTRITION: Calories320, Total Fat 5. 5g, Saturated Fat 3. 5g, Cholesterol 1mg, Sodium 582mg, Total Carbohydrate 50.7g, Dietary Fiber 17. 6g, Total Sugars 7g, Protein 17. 5g

SOUPS AND STEWS

32. Creamy Celery Soup

Preparation Time: 40 minutes

Cooking Time: 15-60 minutes

Servings: 4

INGREDIENTS

- 6 cups celery
- ½ tsp dill
- 2 cups water
- 1 cup coconut milk
- 1 onion, chopped
- Pinch of salt

DIRECTIONS

1. Add all ingredients into the electric pot and stir well.
2. Cover electric pot with the lid and select soup setting.
3. Release pressure using a quick release method than open the lid.
4. Puree the soup using an immersion blender until smooth and creamy.
5. Stir well and serve warm.

NUTRITION: Calories 174; Fat 14.6 g; Carbohydrates 10.5 g; Sugar 5.2 g; Protein 2.8 g; Cholesterol 0 mg

33. Avocado Cucumber Soup

Preparation Time: 40 minutes

Cooking Time: 15-60 minutes

Servings: 3

INGREDIENTS

- 1 large cucumber, peeled and sliced
- ¾ cup water
- ¼ cup lemon juice
- 2 garlic cloves
- 6 green onion
- 2 avocados, pitted
- ½ tsp black pepper
- ½ tsp pink salt

DIRECTIONS

1. Add all ingredients into the blender and blend until smooth and creamy.
2. Place in refrigerator for 30 minutes.
3. Stir well and serve chilled.

NUTRITION: Calories 73; Fat 3.7 g; Carbohydrates 9.2 g; Sugar 2.8 g; Protein 2.2 g; Cholesterol 0 mg

34. Creamy Garlic Onion Soup

Preparation Time: 45 minutes

Cooking Time: 15-60 minutes

Servings: 4

INGREDIENTS

- 1 onion, sliced
- 4 cups vegetable stock
- 1 1/2 tbsp olive oil
- 1 shallot, sliced
- 2 garlic clove, chopped
- 1 leek, sliced
- Salt

DIRECTIONS

1. Add stock and olive oil in a saucepan and bring to boil.
2. Add remaining ingredients and stir well.
3. Cover and simmer for 25 minutes.
4. Puree the soup using an immersion blender until smooth.
5. Stir well and serve warm.

NUTRITION: Calories 90; Fat 7.4 g; Carbohydrates 10.1 g; Sugar 4.1 g; Protein 1 g; Cholesterol 0 mg

35. Avocado Broccoli Soup

Preparation Time: 25 minutes

Cooking Time: 15-60 minutes

Servings: 4

INGREDIENTS

- 2 cups broccoli florets, chopped
- 5 cups vegetable broth
- 2 avocados, chopped
- Pepper
- Salt

DIRECTIONS

1. Cook broccoli in boiling water for 5 minutes. Drain well.
2. Add broccoli, vegetable broth, avocados, pepper, and salt to the blender and blend until smooth.
3. Stir well and serve warm.

NUTRITION: Calories 269; Fat 21.5 g; Carbohydrates 12.8 g; Sugar 2.1 g; Protein 9.2 g; Cholesterol 0 mg

SNACKS

36. Quinoa Broccoli Tots

Preparation Time: 10 minutes

Cooking Time: 20 minutes

Servings: 16

INGREDIENTS

- 2 tablespoons quinoa flour
- 2 cups steamed and chopped broccoli florets
- 1/2 cup nutritional yeast
- 1 teaspoon garlic powder
- 1 teaspoon miso paste
- 2 flax eggs
- 2 tablespoons hummus

DIRECTIONS

1. Place all the ingredients in a bowl, stir until well combined, and then shape the mixture into sixteen small balls.
2. Arrange the balls on a baking sheet lined with parchment paper, spray with oil and bake at 400 degrees F for 20 minutes until brown, turning halfway.
3. When done, let the tots cool for 10 minutes and then serve straight away.

NUTRITION: Calories: 19 Cal Fat: 0 g Carbs: 2 g Protein: 1 g Fiber: 0.5 g

37. Spicy Roasted Chickpeas

Preparation Time: 10 minutes

Cooking Time: 20 minutes

Servings: 6

INGREDIENTS

- 30 ounces cooked chickpeas
- ½ teaspoon salt
- 2 teaspoons mustard powder
- ½ teaspoon cayenne pepper
- 2 tablespoons olive oil

DIRECTIONS

1. Place all the ingredients in a bowl and stir until well coated and then spread the chickpeas in an even layer on a baking sheet greased with oil.
2. Bake the chickpeas for 20 minutes at 400 degrees F until golden brown and crispy and then serve straight away.

NUTRITION: Calories: 187.1 Cal Fat: 7.4 g Carbs: 24.2 g Protein: 7.3 g Fiber: 6.3 g

38. Nacho Kale Chips

Preparation Time: 10 minutes

Cooking Time: 14 hours

Servings: 10

INGREDIENTS

- 2 bunches of curly kale
- 2 cups cashews, soaked, drained
- 1/2 cup chopped red bell pepper
- 1 teaspoon garlic powder
- 1 teaspoon salt
- 2 tablespoons red chili powder
- 1/2 teaspoon smoked paprika
- 1/2 cup nutritional yeast
- 1 teaspoon cayenne
- 3 tablespoons lemon juice
- 3/4 cup water

DIRECTIONS

1. Place all the ingredients except for kale in a food processor and pulse for 2 minutes until smooth.
2. Place kale in a large bowl, pour in the blended mixture, mix until coated, and dehydrate for 14 hours at 120 degrees F until crispy.
3. If dehydrator is not available, spread kale between two baking sheets and bake for 90 minutes at 225 degrees F until crispy, flipping halfway.
4. When done, let chips cool for 15 minutes and then serve.

NUTRITION: Calories: 191 Cal Fat: 12 g Carbs: 16 g Protein: 9 g Fiber: 2 g

DESSERT

39. Mixed Nut Chocolate Fudge

Preparation Time: 15-30 minutes

Cooking Time:2 hours 10 minutes

Servings: 4

INGREDIENTS

- 3 cups unsweetened chocolate chips
- ¼ cup thick coconut milk
- 1 ½ tsp vanilla extract
- A pinch salt
- 1 cup chopped mixed nuts

DIRECTIONS

1. Line a 9-inch square pan with baking paper and set aside.
2. Melt the chocolate chips, coconut milk, and vanilla in a medium pot over low heat.
3. Mix in the salt and nuts until well distributed and pour the mixture into the square pan.
4. Refrigerate for at least for at least 2 hours.
5. Remove from the fridge, cut into squares and serve.

NUTRITION: Calories 907 Fats 31 5g Carbs 152 1g Protein 7. 7g

40. Fruits Stew

Preparation Time: 10 minutes

Cooking Time: 10 minutes

Servings: 4

INGREDIENTS

- 1 avocado, peeled, pitted and sliced
- 1 cup plums, stoned and halved
- 2 cups water
- 2 teaspoons vanilla extract
- 1 tablespoon lemon juice
- 2 tablespoons stevia

DIRECTIONS

1. In a pan, combine the avocado with the plums, water and the other ingredients, bring to a simmer and cook over medium heat for 10 minutes.
2. Divide the mix into bowls and serve cold.

NUTRITION: Calories 178, Fat 4.4, Fiber 2, Carbs 3, Protein 5

41. Avocado and Rhubarb Salad

Preparation Time: 10 minutes

Cooking Time: 0 minutes

Servings: 4

INGREDIENTS

- 1 tablespoon stevia
- 1 cup rhubarb, sliced and boiled
- 2 avocados, peeled, pitted and sliced
- 1 teaspoon vanilla extract
- Juice of 1 lime

DIRECTIONS

1. In a bowl, combine the rhubarb with the avocado and the other ingredients, toss and serve.

NUTRITION: Calories 140, Fat 2, Fiber 2, Carbs 4, Protein 4

42. Plums and Nuts Bowls

Preparation Time: 5 minutes

Cooking Time: 0 minutes

Servings: 2

INGREDIENTS

- 2 tablespoons stevia
- 1 cup walnuts, chopped
- 1 cup plums, pitted and halved
- 1 teaspoon vanilla extract

DIRECTIONS

1. In a bowl, mix the plums with the walnuts and the other ingredients, toss, divide into 2 bowls and serve cold.

NUTRITION: Calories 400, Fat 23, Fiber 4, Carbs 6, Protein 7

43. Avocado and Strawberries Salad

Preparation Time: 5 minutes

Cooking Time: 0 minutes

Servings: 4

INGREDIENTS

- 2 avocados, pitted, peeled and cubed
- 1 cup strawberries, halved
- Juice of 1 lime
- 1 teaspoon almond extract
- 2 tablespoons almonds, chopped
- 1 tablespoon stevia

DIRECTIONS

1. In a bowl, combine the avocados with the strawberries, and the other ingredients, toss and serve.

NUTRITION: Calories 150, Fat 3, Fiber 3, Carbs 5, Protein 6

44. Chocolate Watermelon Cups

Preparation Time: 2 hours

Cooking Time: 0 minutes

Servings: 4

INGREDIENTS

- 2 cups watermelon, peeled and cubed
- 1 tablespoon stevia
- 1 cup coconut cream
- 1 tablespoon cocoa powder
- 1 tablespoon mint, chopped

DIRECTIONS

1. In a blender, combine the watermelon with the stevia and the other ingredients, pulse well, divide into cups and keep in the fridge for 2 hours before serving.

NUTRITION: Calories 164, Fat 14.6, Fiber 2.1, Carbs 9.9, Protein 2.1

45. Vanilla Raspberries Mix

Preparation Time: 10 minutes

Cooking Time: 10 minutes

Servings: 4

INGREDIENTS

- 1 cup water
- 1 cup raspberries
- 3 tablespoons stevia
- 1 teaspoon nutmeg, ground
- ½ teaspoon vanilla extract

DIRECTIONS

1. In a pan, combine the raspberries with the water and the other ingredients, toss, cook over medium heat for 10 minutes, divide into bowls and serve.

NUTRITION: Calories 20, Fat 0.4, Fiber 2.1, Carbs 4, Protein 0.4

46. Potato and Artichoke Al Forno

Preparation Time: 5 minutes

Cooking Time: 5 hours

Servings: 5

INGREDIENTS

- ½ pound baby potatoes, scrubbed clean
- 2 large fennel bulbs, peeled and sliced thinly
- 1 14-ounce artichoke hearts in oil
- 1 cup double cream
- Salt and pepper to taste

DIRECTIONS

1. Place all ingredients in the Instant Pot and give a good stir.
2. Close the lid and do not seal the vent.
3. Press the Slow Cook button and adjust the cooking time to 5 hours.

NUTRITION: Calories 258, Total Fat 16g, Saturated Fat 7g, Total Carbs 26g, Net Carbs 16g, Protein 6g, Sugar: 7g, Fiber: 10g, Sodium: 115mg, Potassium: 876mg, Phosphorus: 168mg

47. Mushroom Bourguignon

Preparation Time: 5 minutes

Cooking Time: 5 minutes

Servings: 6

INGREDIENTS

- 2 tablespoons olive oil
- 2 cloves garlic, minced
- 12 shallots, chopped
- 16 ounces dried porcini mushrooms, soaked in water overnight then drained
- 4 portobello mushrooms, sliced
- 16 ounces shiitake mushrooms, sliced
- 16 ounces chestnut mushrooms, sliced
- 1 medium carrot, sliced
- 1 sprig fresh thyme
- 2 bay leaves
- 1 cup red wine
- 2 tablespoons tomato paste
- Salt and pepper to taste

DIRECTIONS

1. Press the Sauté button on the Instant Pot and heat the oil.
2. Sauté the garlic and shallots until fragrant. Stir in the mushrooms and sauté for 3 minutes.
3. Add in the rest of the ingredients.
4. Close the lid and set the vent to the Sealing position.

5. Press the Pressure Cook or Manual button and adjust the cooking time to 5 minutes.
6. Do natural pressure release.

NUTRITION: Calories 346, Total Fat 6g, Saturated Fat 0.8g, Total Carbs 76g, Net Carbs 64g, Protein 12g, Sugar: 9g, Fiber: 12g, Sodium: 26mg, Potassium: 1662mg, Phosphorus: 337mg

48. Aubergine Penne Arrabbiata

Preparation Time: 5 minutes

Cooking Time: 15 minutes

Servings: 6

INGREDIENTS

- 2 tablespoons olive oil
- 4 cloves garlic, minced
- 12 fresh mixed color chilis, chopped
- 2 aubergines, sliced
- 6 ounces dried whole wheat penne
- 1 14-ounce can plum tomatoes
- 3 tablespoons nutritional yeast
- ½ cup water
- salt and pepper to taste

DIRECTIONS

1. Press the Sauté button on the Instant Pot and heat the olive oil.
2. Sauté the garlic and chilis for 1 minute until lightly toasted.
3. Stir in the aubergines for 2 minutes.
4. Add in the rest of the ingredients and scrape the bottom to remove the brown bits at the bottom.
5. Close the lid and set the vent to the Sealing position.
6. Press the Pressure Cook or Manual button and adjust the cooking time to 10 minutes,
7. Do natural pressure release.

NUTRITION: Calories 291, Total Fat 8g, Saturated Fat 2g, Total Carbs 40g, Net Carbs 35g, Protein 17g, Sugar: 16g, Fiber: 5g, Sodium: 1044mg, Potassium: 579mg, Phosphorus: 290mg

49. Green Beans Ala Trapanese

Preparation Time: 5 minutes

Cooking Time: 14 minutes

Servings: 4

INGREDIENTS

- 1 cup blanched almond
- 2 tablespoons olive oil
- 1 clove of garlic, minced
- 2 cups ripe cherry tomatoes, chopped
- 2 cups green beans
- salt and pepper to taste
- ½ cup pecorino cheese
- 1 bunch fresh basil
- 1 cup rocket arugula

DIRECTIONS

1. Press the Sauté button on the Instant Pot and toast the almond for 3 minutes until lightly golden. Set aside to cool. Once cool, place in a plastic bag and crush with a rolling pan.
2. With the Sauté button still on, heat the oil and sauté the garlic until fragrant.
3. Stir in the tomatoes for 3 minutes or until wilted.
4. Add in the green beans and season with salt and pepper to taste.
5. Close the lid and set the vent to the Sealing position.
6. Press the Pressure Cook or Manual button and adjust the cooking time to 6 minutes.

7. Do quick pressure release.

8. Once the lid is open, press the Sauté button and stir in the pecorino cheese, basil, arugula, and ground almond. Cook for another 3 minutes.

NUTRITION: Calories 128, Total Fat 11g, Saturated Fat 3g, Total Carbs 5g, Net Carbs 3g, Protein 4g, Sugar: 1g, Fiber: 2g, Sodium: 118mg, Potassium: 137mg, Phosphorus: 81mg

50. Indian Spinach

Preparation Time: 5 minutes

Cooking Time: 7 minutes

Servings: 2

INGREDIENTS

- 1 tablespoon olive oil
- 1 teaspoon black mustard seed
- 1 teaspoon cumin seeds
- 1 onion, chopped
- 1 1-inch ginger, sliced
- 1 teaspoon curry powder
- ½ cup coconut cream
- 1-pound baby spinach
- Juice from ½ lemon
- salt and pepper to taste

DIRECTIONS

1. Press the Sauté button on the Instant Pot and heat the oil. Toast the mustard seeds and cumin seeds. Stir in the onion and ginger until fragrant.
2. Add in the rest of the ingredients.
3. Close the lid and set the vent to the Sealing position.
4. Press the Pressure Cook or Manual button and adjust the cooking time to 5 minutes.
5. Do natural pressure release.

NUTRITION: Calories 348, Total Fat 29g, Saturated Fat 19g, Total Carbs 20g, Net Carbs 12g, Protein 10g, Sugar: 4g, Fiber: 8g, Sodium: 187mg, Potassium: 1596mg, Phosphorus: 219mg

CONCLUSION

To conclude, I think it's fair to say that a plant based diet is the healthiest way to live and eat. It will improve your physical and mental health, help you lose weight, prevent chronic diseases like heart disease or cancer, and decrease your risk of diabetes.

It is also highly recommended to become more active and exercise regularly. Not only will this improve your health immensely but it'll also make you feel better and look better. Aim to do a variety of different exercises so that you can improve the strength in your whole body, rather than focusing on one part. As I mentioned above, it's all about balance.

As for the animals, as long as we keep eating them, they will suffer. So if you want to stop supporting the meat, egg and dairy industry and stop eating animals altogether, remember to make a difference by showing people why this is important. Listening to people's arguments and then pointing out where they're wrong or just plain wrong won't change anything. It's not about who has the most valid arguments but about sharing knowledge and spreading awareness.

Don't think that a plant based diet is hard and that you'll always have to eat the same thing. A lot of people say they are getting bored of eating the same thing all the time but I've never been able to understand this mentality. I love trying new foods and recipes, cooking with my family and friends and going out to try new restaurants. I also love cooking new and exciting things so I never feel like I'm missing out on anything.

If you have the right mindset, eating a healthy plant based diet is totally possible and there are several people who are able to do it. And if you can't or you just don't want to, just try cutting back on the meat, dairy, eggs and fish. Reducing your animal product intake will still make a difference for both your health and the animals' lives.

Even if you aren't ready to completely cut meat, fish, eggs or dairy from your diet, there are many methods you can incorporate more plant based meals in your diet.

Try adding more vegetables to your meals instead of meat. Some vegetables like broccoli, kale and spinach are good sources of protein and fiber. If you're vegetarian but want to eat meat, asking for a 'meat free' or 'cheese' option is always a good idea. You should try not to be discouraged if you can't find something listed as vegan on the menu.

Try making your own plant based versions of your favorite dishes or recipes.

A plant-based diet may be healthier and more sustainable than eating meat, but most American consumers are not aware of the associated benefits. It takes time for a new food trend to permeate into society at large, so there is still plenty of room to educate people about the benefits of veganism.

Plant-based diets provide greater health benefits than meat-based diets. In general, a plant-based diet provides more micronutrients and fiber and is more eco-friendly. They also promote a healthier body weight, reduce the risk of heart disease, diabetes, and hypertension, may lower cancer risk in certain cases, and can even prevent the onset of such illnesses if adopted early enough. The primary obstacle to adoption is cost: meat is cheaper than vegan alternatives. The recent increase in veganism makes it seem like a growing trend.

CPSIA information can be obtained
at www.ICGtesting.com
Printed in the USA
BVHW091148150621
609530BV00013B/2623